This book belongs to:

_____

_____

Date of Event

My favorite photo from the event

Guest: Emily McDonald   Key #16
Message: phone: 774-276-6094

Guest: Farnaz Bakhshi   key #6
Message: 562) 631-6859
         Farnazbakhshi @gmail.com

Guest: Lauren Riedel   Key #13
Message: phone 201 566 6769
         serenity523 @gmail.com

Guest: Kimberly Quick Key 40

Message: 408-497-5900

Guest: Faith Cummings Key #47

Message:

Guest: Caitlin Gillespie Key # 49

Message:

585-944-4674

Guest: Eve Stevens   Key #8

Message: I'm married to Mark. we have 2 year old twins!

Guest: JES CARON   Key# 17   Jescaron@outlook.co

Message:

Guest: _____

Message:

Guest:_____

Message:

Guest:_____

Message:

Guest:_____

Message:

Guest:_____

Message:

Guest:_____

Message:

Guest:_____

Message:

Guest:_____

Message:

Guest:_____

Message:

Guest:_____

Message:

Guest:_____

Message:

Guest:_____

Message:

Guest:_____

Message:

Guest:_____

Message:

Guest:_____

Message:

Guest:_____

Message:

Guest:_____

Message:

Guest:_____

Message:

Guest:_____

Message:

Guest:_____

Message:

Guest:_____

Message:

Guest:_____

Message:

Guest:_____

Message:

Guest:_____

Message:

Guest:_____

Message:

Guest:_____

Message:

Guest:_____

Message:

Guest:_____

Message:

Guest:_____

Message:

Guest:_____

Message:

Guest:_____

Message:

Guest:_____

Message:

Guest:_____

Message:

Guest:_____

Message:

Guest:_____

Message:

Guest:_____

Message:

Guest:_____

Message:

Guest:_____

Message:

Guest:_____

Message:

Guest:_____

Message:

Guest:_____

Message:

Guest:_____

Message:

Guest:_____

Message:

Guest:_____

Message:

Guest:_____

Message:

Guest:_____

Message:

Guest:_____

Message:

Guest:_____

Message:

Guest:_____

Message:

Guest:_____

Message:

Guest:_____

Message:

Guest:_____

Message:

Guest:_____

Message:

Guest:_____

Message:

Guest:_____

Message:

Guest:_____

Message:

Guest:_____

Message:

Guest:_____

Message:

Guest:_____

Message:

Guest:_____

Message:

Guest:_____

Message:

Guest:_____

Message:

Guest:_____

Message:

Guest:_____

Message:

Guest:_____

Message:

Guest:_____

Message:

Guest:_____

Message:

Guest:_____

Message:

Guest:_____

Message:

Guest:_____

Message:

Guest:_____

Message:

Guest:_____

Message:

Guest:_____

Message:

Guest:_____

Message:

Guest:_____

Message:

Guest:_____

Message:

Guest:_____

Message:

Guest:_____

Message:

Guest:_____

Message:

Guest:_____

Message:

Guest:_____

Message:

Guest:_____

Message:

Guest:_____

Message:

Guest:_____

Message:

Guest:_____

Message:

Guest:_____

Message:

Guest:_____

Message:

Guest:_____

Message:

Guest:_____

Message:

Guest:_____

Message:

Guest:_____

Message:

Guest:_____

Message:

Guest:_____

Message:

Guest:_____

Message:

Guest:_____

Message:

Guest:_____

Message:

Guest:_____

Message:

Guest:_____

Message:

Guest:_____

Message:

Guest:_____

Message:

Guest:_____

Message:

Guest:_____

Message:

Guest:_____

Message:

Guest:_____

Message:

Guest:_____

Message:

Guest:_____

Message:

Guest:_____

Message:

Guest:_____

Message:

Guest:_____

Message:

Guest:_____

Message:

Guest:_____

Message:

Guest:_____

Message:

Guest:_____

Message:

Guest:_____

Message:

Guest:_____

Message:

Guest:_____

Message:

Guest:_____

Message:

Guest:_____

Message:

Guest:_____

Message:

Guest:_____

Message:

Guest:_____

Message:

Guest:_____

Message:

Guest:_____

Message:

Guest:_____

Message:

Guest:_____

Message:

Guest:_____

Message:

Guest:_____

Message:

Guest:_____

Message:

Guest:_____

Message:

Guest:_____

Message:

Guest:_____

Message:

Guest:_____

Message:

Guest:_____

Message:

Guest:_____

Message:

Guest:_____

Message:

Guest:_____

Message:

Guest:_____

Message:

Guest:_____

Message:

Guest:_____

Message:

Guest:_____

Message:

Guest:_____

Message:

Guest:_____

Message:

Guest:_____

Message:

Guest:_____

Message:

Guest:_____

Message:

Gifts I Received:

Guest Name:	Gift Received:	Thank You Card Sent?

Gifts I Received:

Guest Name:	Gift Received:	Thank You Card Sent?

Gifts I Received:

Guest Name:	Gift Received:	Thank You Card Sent?

Gifts I Received:

Guest Name:	Gift Received:	Thank You Card Sent?

Gifts I Received:

Guest Name:	Gift Received:	Thank You Card Sent?

Gifts I Received:

Guest Name:	Gift Received:	Thank You Card Sent?

Gifts I Received:

Guest Name:	Gift Received:	Thank You Card Sent?

Gifts I Received:

Guest Name:	Gift Received:	Thank You Card Sent?

Gifts I Received:

Guest Name:	Gift Received:	Thank You Card Sent?

Gifts I Received:

Guest Name:	Gift Received:	Thank You Card Sent?

My favorite memories from the Party:

_____

_____

_____

_____

_____

_____

_____

_____

_____

_____

_____

_____

_____

My favorite memories from the Party:

_____

_____

_____

_____

_____

_____

_____

_____

_____

_____

_____

My favorite memories from the Party:

_____

_____

_____

_____

_____

_____

_____

_____

_____

_____

_____

_____

My favorite memories from the Party:

_____

_____

_____

_____

_____

_____

_____

_____

_____

_____

_____

_____

_____

My favorite memories from the Party:

_____

_____

_____

_____

_____

_____

_____

_____

_____

_____

_____

_____

_____

_____

My favorite memories from the Party:

_____

_____

_____

_____

_____

_____

_____

_____

_____

_____

_____

_____

My favorite memories from the Party:

_____

_____

_____

_____

_____

_____

_____

_____

_____

_____

_____

_____

My favorite memories from the Party:

_____

_____

_____

_____

_____

_____

_____

_____

_____

_____

_____

My favorite memories from the Party:

_____

_____

_____

_____

_____

_____

_____

_____

_____

_____

_____

_____

_____

My favorite memories from the Party:

_____

_____

_____

_____

_____

_____

_____

_____

_____

_____

_____

_____

Made in the USA
Middletown, DE
27 September 2019